Frankenstein

Mary Shelley

adapted by Philip Pullman

OXFORD

UNIVERSITY PRESS

OXFORD
UNIVERSITY PRESS

Great Clarendon Street, Oxford OX2 6DP

Oxford University Press is a department of the University of Oxford.
It furthers the University's objective of excellence in research,
scholarship, and education by publishing worldwide in

Oxford New York

Auckland Cape Town Dar es Salaam Hong Kong Karachi
Kuala Lumpur Madrid Melbourne Mexico City Nairobi
New Delhi Shanghai Taipei Toronto

With offices in

Argentina Austria Brazil Chile Czech Republic France Greece
Guatemala Hungary Italy Japan Poland Portugal Singapore
South Korea Switzerland Thailand Turkey Ukraine Vietnam

Oxford is a registered trade mark of Oxford University Press
in the UK and in certain other countries

British Library Cataloguing in Publication Data

Data available

ISBN 978 0 19 831498 1

30 29 28 27 26 25 24

MIX
Paper from
responsible sources
FSC
www.fsc.org   FSC® C007785

Printed and bound by Bell & Bain Ltd, Glasgow

Acknowledgements
The Publisher would like to thank the following for permission to
reproduce photographs:
Hulton Archive: page 62;
Polka Children's Theatre: page 72 (both).

Illustrations are by Jonathon Heap.

Cover image © AF archive/Alamy

The Publisher would like to thank Jenny Roberts for writing the Activities section.

Recommended Edition
Mary Shelley, *Frankenstein*. Oxford World's Classics, OUP, 2008

Contents

General Introduction

With a fresh, modern look, this classroom-friendly series boasts an exciting range of authors – from Pratchett to Chaucer – whose works have been expertly adapted by such well-known and popular writers as Philip Pullman and David Calcutt.

Many teachers use Oxford *Playscripts* to study the format, style, and structure of playscripts with their students; for speaking and listening assignments; to initiate discussion of relevant issues in class; to cover Drama as part of the curriculum; as an introduction to the novel of the same title; and to introduce the less able or willing to pre-1914 literature.

At the back of each Oxford *Playscript*, you will find a brand new Activity section, which not only addresses the points above, but also features close text analysis, and activities that provide support for underachieving readers and act as a springboard for personal writing.

Many schools will simply read through the play in class with no staging at all, and the Activity sections have been written with this in mind, with individual activities ranging from debates and designing campaign posters to writing extra scenes or converting parts of the original novels into playscript form.

For those of you, however, who do wish to take to the stage, we have included, where necessary, 'A Note on Staging' – a section dedicated to suggesting ways of staging the play, as well as examining the props and sets you may wish to use.

Above all, we hope you will enjoy using Oxford *Playscripts*, be it on the stage or in the classroom.

What the Adapter Says

Frankenstein is a story about what it means to be human. One of the things that makes us human (perhaps *the* thing) is language, and the Monster's increasing command of language is one of the things which any production needs to bring out.

In the book, the Monster himself tells a lot of the story. He tells how he finds the cottage in the forest, and hides nearby, listening to the family through the wall and learning, little by little, how to understand them.

In a play, though, it is not possible to show things happening gradually over a long period. You have to find dramatic moments, single incidents that arise from what's gone before and set the course for what will happen next. So, in Act 3, the Monster is already able to speak at least as well as Frankenstein. His long speeches are very important, and they should be spoken clearly, passionately, and powerfully, as a brilliant lawyer speaks in court. If the actor playing the Monster has gained the audience's sympathy in the previous Acts, they will listen to the speeches with close attention.

Something I wanted to get away from in this play was the lurching, lumpish monster, hands outstretched, that everyone can imitate jokingly. Mary Shelley, in the novel, stresses the Monster's athleticism and speed, and after all Frankenstein created him to be powerful and active. If the Monster looks as ugly as a corpse, but moves with the grace and energy of a dancer or gymnast, the effect is electric. Literally!

The final section, with the Monster trying to bring the Bride to life and Frankenstein destroying it, and the other characters dying, must not be taken slowly. The sections must follow each other almost too swiftly for thought, as in a dream, otherwise the tension goes out of it and all the corpses piling up look merely funny.

One major change I made was to have the blind person, whom the Monster tries to befriend, a young woman instead of an old man. In the book, there are three people in the cottage: Felix, Agathe, and their blind father. You might feel that in making this change, I was being sexist, and wanting to exploit the contrast between a powerful male monster and a frail, helpless female. On the other hand, you might feel that I was provoking a more interesting role for an actress in a story where women have otherwise very little to do. I know which I think I was doing.

Philip Pullman

A Note on Staging

Costumes and Props

Props you may need include:

Frankenstein:	a heavy coat.
Clerval:	a heavy (over-)coat; a rucksack.
Elizabeth:	a bonnet; a cloak; a portable lamp.
Felix:	a canvas bag; a 'dead rabbit'; a musket, a ramrod, shot, and powder.
Agathe:	a basket of mushrooms.
The Monster:	a long, black cloak.
Servant:	2 pistols.

Special Effects

You may wish to consider the following:

Act One:	'showers of sparks and wreaths of smoke' (this could be achieved simply through lighting and/or with dry ice)
	the sound of thunder (this could be created with drums)
Act Two:	birdsong (a pre-recording or percussion might be used to good effect)
	dogs barking (a recording might come in useful here)
Act Four:	electrical noise, 'a powerful humming and crackling' (you could create this effect with a variety of percussion instruments)

The Play at a Glance

The outline of the play below highlights the props or scenery you may want to consider for a performance.

Prologue *The Arctic – 'A landscape of bright snow and ice'*
This scene could simply be staged with a simple spotlight on Captain Walton.

Act One *Frankenstein's room in Ingolstadt*

High, arched windows (which ideally can be opened and closed); a door; a long wire (leading from outside the window); a lamp; many 'phials and bottles' on shelves; a 'large electrical-looking machine'; a bench; a sheet; a 'complicated piece of apparatus'; an armchair; a cushion; a 'human thigh bone'; a bottle of wine; a glass; a fireplace; a 'flint and steel'; a chair; a 'Wimshurst machine' (see page 16 for a full description); a 'human hand'; a door.

Act Two *The cottage in the forest*

A table; 2 chairs; a fireplace; a window; some bread, cheese, and an apple; 2 doors (one upstage, another to one side; guitar; a 'portrait of an elderly man'; logs; a small mirror.

Act Three *Frankenstein's study in Geneva*

A window (with shutters); a lamp; a fireplace with fire; 2 chairs; a table; a trapdoor (optional).

Act Four *Frankenstein's study in Geneva*

As above, plus: a bench; a sheet; a 'large electrical machine … as tall as a man'; lots of wires; a large knife.

Epilogue *The Arctic – 'A landscape of bright snow and ice'*

As Prologue.

Characters

Captain Walton	an Arctic explorer; tough, bearded, wearing furs; a man who has been in many dangerous places and survived, but who has come across something now that has shaken him to the depths
Frankenstein	young and idealistic; a dreamer, full of strange ideas, who believes that his work will improve the world
Clerval	the same age as **Frankenstein**; realistic and humorous, he is impressed by his friend's achievements but anxious about their effects
Landlady	middle-aged, probably, but it doesn't matter
Elizabeth	a year or two younger than **Frankenstein**; she is devoted to his father and to **William**, and she loves **Frankenstein** without understanding him
The Monster	should look hideous – he is made of corpses, after all; very strong and agile, and, although when he first comes to life he cannot move easily, it makes him much more impressive in the later Acts if he is graceful and powerful and does not lurch about clumsily; his voice should be impressive
Felix	young, quick-tempered, fiery; he and **Agathe** are political refugees
Agathe	blind, but she should move about the room as easily as a sighted person; she knows the room well, knows where everything is; it is when she first becomes aware that something is wrong that she begins to look vulnerable
Ghost of William	best played in a dead white mask, to give the effect of something or someone not quite alive
The Monster's Bride	should be as hideous as the **Monster** is; when he first sees her, he is shocked
Servant	male

Prologue

The Arctic. A landscape of bright snow and ice.

*Enter **Captain Walton**, clothed in furs.*

He speaks quietly, thoughtfully, as if recollecting a deep experience.

Captain Walton   Some time ago, I had the command of a ship on an expedition to the Arctic Circle. We sailed further north than anyone had ever gone before, and then there came a day when we could go no further, because the ice had closed us in. Weeks went by; months passed, and still we couldn't move. Strange things happen to your mind in those regions of eternal snow. The sailors began to report seeing things, impossible things, and hearing voices in the empty air – one voice like someone crying in pain or anguish, another voice that was deep and harsh and monstrous, howling of revenge; I began to worry that they'd go mad with fear, crazy with isolation; I began to suspect that there were ghosts in the air, evil spirits behind the bright light glaring on the snow … And then I saw it myself, and I could doubt no longer. In the distance, a sledge was moving across the ice, pulled by a team of dogs, and driving it was a creature like a man, but huge and hideous beyond belief. And pursuing it – always in pursuit but never catching up – was a man on foot. We watched from the deck, the sailors and I, and then the man fell down and lay still on the snow. I sent out a party to bring him in. He told us that his name was … Frankenstein. We laid him in my cabin and looked after him, and presently he'd recovered enough to tell us his story. And a strange one it was …

He exits quietly.

*As he goes off, the light fades and the curtain rises to show **Frankenstein's** room in Ingolstadt for Act One.*

Act 1

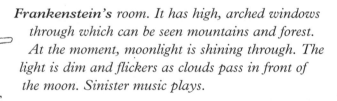

Frankenstein's room. It has high, arched windows through which can be seen mountains and forest. At the moment, moonlight is shining through. The light is dim and flickers as clouds pass in front of the moon. Sinister music plays.

Then a hand reaches down from above, as if from the roof, and pulls the window open from the outside. A second later the shape of a man – Frankenstein – is seen to climb athletically down the outside and in through the window. He brings with him a wire, which seems to be attached to something up on the roof. Because of the dim light in the room it is impossible to be certain what he is doing.

He leans out of the window and calls up softly.

Frankenstein   Clerval! Are you staying up there all night?

There is a scrambling sound offstage, as if the other person is not sure of his footing.

Clerval   *[Off]* I can't find the right place – ah, here it is – where the devil do I put my foot?

A leg can be seen waving uncertainly about, feeling for a foothold. Frankenstein takes it and guides it to safety. A moment later, Clerval appears in the window and jumps down to join Frankenstein. They are both in their early twenties: Frankenstein intense, poetic; Clerval stout, cheerful, matter-of-fact.

Frankenstein lights a lamp. The room is an odd mixture of shabby sitting-room and cluttered laboratory. Phials and bottles of chemicals and preserved specimens of various kinds line the shelves. A large, electrical-looking machine stands in the corner. On a bench at the back lies something – obviously the Monster – covered by a sheet.

11

Clerval rubs his hands with the cold and looks around curiously.

So this is where you lurk, Frankenstein! D'you know, the other students are convinced you're a wizard?

Frankenstein	A wizard! Why's that?

*Both men have heavy coats on. **Clerval** is carrying a rucksack, which he takes off and drops on the floor. **Frankenstein** reacts with nervous anger.*

Frankenstein	Don't drop that!
Clerval	I'm sorry. What's in it? It feels like several pounds of meat.
Frankenstein	Well, it's … just that. Several pounds of meat.
Clerval	I hope it tastes good. Where are you going to cook it? Don't you have a fire in here? It feels as cold as it does outside. Colder, if anything.

Frankenstein is busy adjusting the wire he has brought in, securing it to brackets around the walls, and leading it to the bench.

Frankenstein	No. No fire. I keep it cold on purpose – it's the only way to preserve my specimens … I don't notice it any more. Hold this, would you …

*Gives the end of the wire to **Clerval**, then goes back and props the window open.*

Clerval	You're not going to leave it open? We'll freeze to death, man!
Frankenstein	You'll get used to it. The only problem comes when you have to do delicate work with your hands … There. That should fix it.

He stands back, surveying the arrangement of the wire.

Clerval	Remarkable. Extraordinary. A phenomenon. I congratulate you, Frankenstein. Now what the devil's it all about? You bring me clambering over the rooftops carrying our next week's suppers in a rucksack; suppers which, by the way, you intend to eat raw, since you don't go in for lighting fires; you fix a length of copper wire to the highest point of the house, and

	trail it all the way down here and leave me holding the end of it – what's it all about, Frankenstein?
Frankenstein	My dear fellow! Let me take it from you …
	Takes the end of the wire and fastens it to a complicated piece of apparatus near the bench.
	There. Now you won't explode.
	Clerval steps away hastily.
Clerval	Explode?
Frankenstein	A joke. *[Solemnly]* Ha ha ha.
Clerval	Oh, a joke! I see. Ha ha.
Frankenstein	Sit down, Clerval, there's a good man. If you really want a fire, I suppose lighting one just this once won't make any difference. And to tell the truth, I feel like celebrating. D'you think there's going to be a storm?
Clerval	A storm? Oh, bound to be.
	He sits in an armchair, then sits upright quickly and feels behind him. He brings out a human thigh-bone from behind the cushion and stares at it with distaste.
	Last night's supper? Or this morning's breakfast?
Frankenstein	So that's where it got to …
	He takes it, puts it on a shelf, and brings down a bottle of wine from which he pulls the cork by hand.
Frankenstein	There's a glass on the floor beside the chair, Clerval. I've only got the one. We'll share it.
	Clerval finds it. It's dirty and covered in dust. Frankenstein rubs it on his sleeve before pouring the wine in.
Frankenstein	Your good health!
	Drinks deeply, fills the glass again, walks upstage, leaving Clerval waiting for his turn.

Yes, if we're lucky tonight and it storms, and if my wire does the job it's supposed to, and if … well, my dear fellow, we're on the threshold of a new age.

Clerval   You don't say?

Frankenstein   There's no harm in telling you. It's bound to come out sooner or later, and you're an intelligent man. You'll understand …

Clerval   Kind of you. The wine, Frankenstein …

Frankenstein   Ah! Forgive me.

*Pours another glass, takes it to **Clerval**.*

Yes – my work. So they call me a wizard, do they? Perhaps they're not far wide of the mark. I expect two hundred years ago they'd have burnt me at the stake.

Clerval   Not a bad idea. Then we could have warmed ourselves up …

Rubs his hands, shivers …

Frankenstein   All right, all right. I'll light the fire.

He crosses to the grate. As he does so, there is a distant rumble of thunder. He stops and looks out, with an expression of satisfaction.

Hear that? It's way over the mountains just yet, but it's on its way …

*He stoops, strikes a flint and steel, and starts a fire in the grate. **Clerval** huddles closer to it as **Frankenstein** goes to the window to peer out.*

Frankenstein   Another hour or so, I should think. You can see the lightning playing around the peaks.

Clerval	All right, let me guess. Storm – lightning – wire – electricity.
Frankenstein	Very good!
Clerval	Electricity … Umm … Magnetism? You've invented a way of making magnets?
Frankenstein	Nothing like it.

He comes to sit in the other chair, takes the wine glass and fills it again.

	Frogs' legs.
Clerval	And the same to you. Or is that the menu?
Frankenstein	No! An Italian called Galvani – heard of him?
Clerval	I'm a philosopher, not a musician. All Italian composers sound the same to me.
Frankenstein	Nothing to do with music. He was a scientist, Clerval. A natural philosopher. He was dissecting a frog one day, and he found that the nerve in the leg responded to electricity. It twitched when a current passed through it.
Clerval	Now I have heard about that, come to think of it. He thought there was a kind of animal electricity, didn't he? And is that what you're working on?
Frankenstein	More or less. But there's no such thing as animal electricity – it's all one. The same force flows in your nerves as in the frog's, and the very same force flows through the lightning … Did I ever tell you how I first realized what my life's work was to be? I was fourteen years old, at home in Geneva, on a night like this – a storm was threatening. They rise very quickly in the mountains there. Outside our front door, about twenty yards away, stood a great old oak tree. It had been there for three hundred years at least, and it was still green and strong. I'd climbed it, I'd sheltered under it, I'd carved my initials on the trunk … and just as the storm was at its height, I opened the door to look at the lightning. You've never seen such a storm! The tree was lit up bright, bright green by flash after

15

flash, and the thunder was exploding around the house like artillery fire. Then without any warning the tree was engulfed in flame. A colossal blaze shot right out of it, all in a moment, and dazzled me so I could hardly see ... When I opened my eyes again, only a moment later, the tree was gone. There was nothing there at all but a charred, smoking stump. That great living thing, smashed to atoms in an instant! And I thought: the power that can do that is the power of life and death. I'll harness it. I'll study it and master it and make it work for mankind.

Clerval   I see. And now you've done it?

Frankenstein   Nearly. Nearly, Clerval!

*Drains the glass, fills it again, hands it to **Clerval**.*

Clerval   So ... you're going to collect some electricity from the lightning and bring it down here, and ... what then?

Frankenstein   And then ... drink the wine.

***Clerval** raises his eyebrows, but drains the glass.*

Clerval   Well?

Frankenstein   And then this happens.

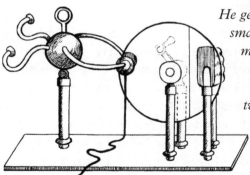

He gets up and goes to the bench. Next to it is a smaller trolley on wheels, on which is mounted a machine consisting of two glass discs that rotate in opposite directions when turned by a handle. Attached to a brass terminal is a twisted piece of wire that leads down to something on a slab of marble, covered at the moment with a cloth.

***Clerval** stands up to come closer and look at it.*

Clerval   Now that I recognize ... it's a what d'ye call it.

Frankenstein   This thing? It's a Wimshurst machine. And I expect you'll

16

recognize this –

*Takes the cloth away. **Clerval** peers, then starts back in disgust.*

Clerval   It's a human hand!

A hand is lying flat on the slab, but we cannot see it clearly. That's what it is, however – yellowed, dried, and withered, and thoroughly revolting.

Where did you get that from?

Frankenstein   From the dissecting room at the University. Quite proper, I assure you. The chap it was attached to was hanged; he had no further use for it. As a matter of fact, he strangled his wife with it only last month.

Clerval   Good grief! Frankenstein, how can you joke about such things?

Frankenstein   Yes, of course, you're right. I'm sorry. It's the excitement, Clerval. I'm so close to … never mind. I'll show you what the machine does, if you're still interested.

Clerval   Of course I'm interested! But I don't care to be ghoulish about it.

Frankenstein   No, no. Heaven forbid.

*He connects the wire to something on the bench, checks that all is ready, and takes the handle of the machine. Before he turns it, he addresses **Clerval**.*

Think of this as … a philosopher should, Clerval. There's no cause for shock or disgust in nature.

Clerval   I wonder. Carry on, then.

*****Frankenstein** begins to turn the handle. The glass discs start rotating slowly in opposite directions; an electric hum fills the air; sparks are seen to jump from one brass terminal to another – all contributing to the impression of high powered electrical activity.*

Frankenstein   There – can you see it? Can you see the finger twitching?

Clerval   *[Leaning over, but not so as to obscure the audience's view]* The index finger – yes! It's definitely moving – and now the thumb

| | – Good God, Frankenstein, it's horrible! |
| Frankenstein | Philosophy, Clerval! Let me increase the charge … |

Turns the handle faster. And suddenly the hand moves so that all the audience can see it: it curves up horribly, palm towards us, fingers curved and twitching. Clerval steps back and gasps.

| Clerval | Ugghh! |
| Frankenstein | No – wait – that knob at the side of the bench – |

He is still turning the handle vigorously, and he nods down in the direction he means. Clerval comes closer, fascinated and horrified.

| Clerval | This one? |
| Frankenstein | Turn it – slowly – when I tell you. Clockwise. |

Clerval reaches for it.

| Frankenstein | Now. *Slowly.* |

Clerval turns it – and the hand slowly clenches.

| Clerval | Good God! |

He turns it back – the hand unclenches again, and stands up from the bench stiff and twitching as before.

| Frankenstein | Again. |

Clerval does it again.

| Clerval | Extraordinary! |
| Frankenstein | That's not all. Let it open again – that's it – now try the lever next to the knob. Gently, gently. I haven't tried this yet. |

Frankenstein is still turning the handle, the glass discs are still revolving, the sparks are still crackling. Clerval reaches for the lever and moves it a fraction, then a bit further – and the forefinger curls forward slowly to meet the thumb. Clerval leans over, as excited as Frankenstein by what he can make the hand do. Like two small boys, they play with it for a moment or two.

Clerval	Look! It can bring its thumb across – let me try the knob at the same time …
Frankenstein	That's it! Just a bit more …
Clerval	And … there! The thumb's touching the little finger! Wonderful!
Frankenstein	Excellent! Now we'll try the –

A flash from the machine, a loud crack, and they start back as the hand falls lifelessly to the bench.

Clerval	What happened?
Frankenstein	The charge. I was turning the handle too fast – it's burnt the wire out, look.

He holds up a charred end of wire. **Clerval** *mops his brow.*

Clerval	Frankenstein, I'm astounded. This is the greatest discovery of the age! A wonderful piece of work!
Frankenstein	A step or two beyond Signor Galvani, eh?
Clerval	It's beyond anything I've ever heard of. When are you going to publish it? The world should be hearing about your genius, my friend! You should be honoured – you should have doctorates, professorships –

Seizes the bottle and glass and pours some wine.

To your fame, Frankenstein!

Drinks deeply, then makes a face.

And I hope you'll buy better wine when you're famous. That's if you want company when you drink it.

Frankenstein covers the hand again with the cloth and wheels the trolley back out of the way as he speaks.

Frankenstein	You're a good fellow, Clerval. That's why I wanted you to see what I'd done. You've no idea how lonely it's been … I've been working at this for six years now. Six years! I mastered the physiology of the hand a long time ago. I could do this

demonstration in my first year of study …

Clerval sits, and Frankenstein comes to join him.

Clerval	You mean there's more?
Frankenstein	That was only the first crude attempt. I took that hand on purpose to show you; I could have shown you four years ago. I … as a matter of fact, I wasn't telling the truth when I said where it came from. I hope you won't mention it to anyone. I … well, I dug it up last night.
Clerval	You *what*?
Frankenstein	I've begged the University for specimens. They say I've had all their best material for years, and produced nothing to show for it. How could I show them that? Can you imagine the reaction? They won't give me anything now. I have to …

He shrugs. Clerval is taken aback.

Clerval	You dig them up? Good Lord, Frankenstein, how many corpses are there without hands in our graveyards?
Frankenstein	Not just hands. D'you think I want to do it this way? I'd far rather have the use of a proper dissecting-room, and all the resources of the University – I have to go without meals to buy the chemicals I need, I have nowhere to store my specimens, my landlady drives me mad with her incessant questions –
Clerval	What d'you mean, *not just hands*? What else –

A thought strikes him suddenly – he looks at the rucksack with horrified suspicion.

What's in there?

Frankenstein	Oh, nothing – that's just –

He gets up anxiously, crosses to where the rucksack is lying – but before he can pick it up, there is a loud knock. He starts nervously.

Landlady	*[Off]* Herr Frankenstein! Are you there?
Frankenstein	*[To Clerval]* My landlady – *[Calling]* Yes, Frau Liebermann?

Landlady	*[Off]* A constable to see you. What's going on, Herr Frankenstein?
Frankenstein	I haven't the faintest idea, Frau Liebermann, probably some silly mistake. I'll come down and see him. *[To **Clerval**]* I'll be back in a minute. Be a good fellow – don't touch anything …
	*He leaves. **Clerval** sits for a moment, thoughtful; then he gets up, crosses to the rucksack, and picks it up, feeling its weight, feeling it through the canvas: then he turns it around, and sees a spreading bloodstain. He drops it with horror.*
Clerval	Good grief …
	He backs away, then goes to the window and looks out.
	Frankenstein, are you mad, or am I? … There's going to be a storm soon, I can feel it.
	He shivers.
	And then what? Lightning … lightning! Electricity! The hand … what on earth?
	*He follows the wire to its destination on the large bench with the sheeted body of the **Monster**. We can see him steeling himself to look.*
	Frankenstein, what have you done?
	He reaches out to pull the sheet down, nervously, when there's a timid knock at the door. He starts guiltily.
	Yes? Yes, who's that?
Elizabeth	*[Off]* Victor? May I come in?
Clerval	It's not Victor – but yes, come in, come in …
	*The door opens and **Elizabeth** comes in, dressed for a journey: bonnet, cloak, etc. She is young, about eighteen, and, at the moment, nervous.*
Elizabeth	I beg your pardon, sir – the landlady said I would find Herr Frankenstein's rooms up here …
Clerval	Yes, that's right. This is his place. I'm a friend of his – Henri

21

de Clerval. He's … I thought he was downstairs at the moment? Seeing a visitor?

Elizabeth	The landlady was not very friendly. I … I'm his cousin, monsieur. I've come a long way.

She sways as if tired or about to faint. **Clerval** *helps her to a chair.*

Clerval	Mademoiselle … please, sit down. I'm sure your cousin won't be long.
Elizabeth	Thank you, monsieur. I'm tired; I've come a long way today. He wasn't expecting me, but there was no time to let him know I was coming …
Clerval	Is there any trouble, mademoiselle? He's never mentioned his family. I thought he was alone in the world.
Elizabeth	His father's very ill. His mother is dead; there's only his father and me and his little brother, and when his father fell ill I wrote to Victor and told him, but he never answered my letters. I didn't know what else to do.
Clerval	He's wrapped up in his researches, I'm afraid. A brilliant man, but … well, you know him, after all. Wasn't he like this when he was a child?
Elizabeth	Yes, I suppose he was. Monsieur de Clerval, is he in trouble?
Clerval	Trouble? Why?
Elizabeth	Something's not right. I'm worried. I have such dreams … I see Victor in them, and there's something horrible pursuing him – or is he pursuing it? But there's such a sense of doom and despair … I'm sorry. I shouldn't be telling you this. Where is Victor now?
Clerval	Seeing a visitor. He won't be long.

Pause. She shivers.

Clerval	You're cold. Let me shut the window.

He crosses to the window. She has her back to him; he sees the wire again, follows it with his eyes to the sheeted figure, and hesitates.

Clerval	Mademoiselle ... have you anywhere to stay? There's a comfortable inn just across the square. I'd be glad to take your luggage across there for you.
Elizabeth	That's kind of you, monsieur. You're right; I can hardly stay here, and Victor isn't expecting me. My valise is in the hall.
Clerval	I'll go and do it now. Your cousin will be up soon, I'm sure ...

He goes out quickly. She sits still for a moment looking weary and anxious.

In the distance there is a rumble of thunder. Startled, she looks around at the window and sees that it is still open. She gets up to close it – and her eye is caught by the sheeted form on the bench. Hesitantly she approaches – reaches out to touch it – is about the pull back the sheet, when the door bursts open and –

Frankenstein	No! Don't touch it!

He runs in and pulls her away, then peers out of the window and up into the sky.

Elizabeth	Victor! Whatever's the matter? What is it?
Frankenstein	Elizabeth – you mustn't stay here. Not now. Where's Clerval?
Elizabeth	He went to take my valise to the inn across the square – but Victor, what's going on? Are you in trouble?
Frankenstein	No, no – but I'm in the middle of a crucial experiment, I can't leave it – you haven't touched anything?
Elizabeth	Not a thing. But Victor – what's the matter with you? I've come all the way from home, I'm tired and cold, I haven't seen you for six months – you haven't even asked me why I'm here.
Frankenstein	I'm sorry ... why *are* you here? Is something wrong?
Elizabeth	It's your father, Victor. He's very ill.
Frankenstein	Oh no ... what is it? How long's he been unwell?

Elizabeth	It's an affliction of the lungs. I wrote to you a month ago, when it first came on, and again a fortnight later, and again last week. What are you doing, Victor? Why don't you answer my letters? You haven't even read them! If you want to see your father alive, you'd better come home tomorrow.
Frankenstein	Tomorrow! But –
Elizabeth	But what? What's more important than that? To him, I mean. I can see there's plenty more important to you. A son who doesn't come when his father's dying … oh, you make me ill. Now I'm going to the inn to find something to eat and go to bed. I'm very tired.

She moves towards the door. He tries to hold her back.

Frankenstein	No, Elizabeth, don't – you're right, I'll come back with you – but my work, you don't understand, it's reached the point I've been working towards for six years –
Elizabeth	Understand? How can I understand a son who cares nothing for his father? How can I understand someone who shuts himself up in a dirty dusty smelly freezing cold room like this, and says that this is more important to him than his family?

He tries to hold her still, but she shakes him off.

Elizabeth	No – don't try to hold me back. If this is what matters to you, Victor, then so be it. I've done my duty – now I'm going to lie down, because I'm tired, and in the morning I shall go back home, whether or not you come with me.

She goes out. He sinks into a chair, despairing.

Frankenstein	Must it finish, then? So close … so nearly ready!

He holds his head in his hands.

After a moment there comes a tremendous clap of thunder – deafening – as if right overhead. **Frankenstein** *sits up at once and stares at the form on the bench. It is quite still. He jumps up and runs to the window, through which we can hear the start of heavy rainfall. He looks out and upwards, and is outlined in a flash of lightning. He looks around again, checking the wire, but still the* *figure lies unmoving. Then comes more thunder – longer and even louder than before.*

*Feverishly he runs to the bench, checks the wire, and folds back the sheet a little way so that he can see the **Monster's** face.*

Frankenstein	It must be tonight – it must be!

A frantic knocking at the door.

Clerval	*[Off]* Frankenstein! Open up! Open up!
Frankenstein	No! Go away, Clerval! I can't be disturbed!
Clerval	Frankenstein, I must talk to you –
Frankenstein	Impossible! Go away, man!

More furious hammering on the door.

Clerval	You must let me in – I know what you're doing, Frankenstein –

***Frankenstein** runs to the door.*

Frankenstein	Clerval, I beg you – leave me alone – you don't know how dangerous this could be –

*But the door bursts open. **Frankenstein** is flung aside as **Clerval** runs in, looks around, and runs to where the **Monster** is lying. He tears off the sheet and flings it to the floor as **Frankenstein** recovers and runs across to tear him away.*

Frankenstein	Don't! Don't touch it! The lightning could strike at any moment –

*They struggle in front of the window, illuminated by another great flash of lightning; and almost at once comes the thunder. They freeze, both looking in apprehension at the bench. Then comes another flash, lighting up the whole room, accompanied by showers of sparks and wreaths of smoke – and on the bench, the **Monster** tenses convulsively.*

Clerval	No!
Frankenstein	Leave it – leave it –

*Another flash, more thunder – and this time the **Monster** really* *comes alive, thrashing from side to side as if trying to sit up. **Clerval** breaks away from **Frankenstein** and stares at it in horror.*

Clerval Frankenstein – what have you created?

Frankenstein I told you not to come in!

Clerval This is pure evil, Frankenstein –

*He starts forward as if to destroy it, but **Frankenstein**, seeing his intention, seizes a chair and strikes him with it from behind. The chair breaks – **Clerval** falls stunned.*

Frankenstein Oh, my friend – you don't know how important it is …

*He runs to the **Monster's** side and tears off the wires, and then helps it to sit up. The storm is still raging outside, and there are flashes of lightning. The **Monster** is enormously tall and powerfully built. His open eyes are hideous, red-rimmed, and glaring in a waxy yellow face. His lips are black, scars criss-cross his cheeks, and his face is framed with matted black hair. He is naked to the waist. He wears nothing but simple breeches.*

*The **Monster** stands there, swaying as **Frankenstein** moves back to get a better look at his creation. Then the **Monster** raises a hand and **Frankenstein** reaches up to touch it.*

My creature! And living! Let me see you – let me look at you – ah …

*He runs his hands over the **Monster's** limbs checking their soundness, helping him balance upright. The **Monster's** eyes follow him, as if confused.*

*Then **Frankenstein** stands back, and a first realization of what he has made passes over him. He shudders.*

But you're not what I thought you'd be … I thought I was making an angel! D'you know that? I thought I was making something better than human! Something so precious and beautiful that everyone would love it – and look at you. Look at what I've done.

*The **Monster** takes a lurching step towards him. **Frankenstein** backs away nervously.*

No! This isn't what I wanted. Oh, dear God, what have I done? Is it alive after all?

*The **Monster** makes a strange noise.*

No! I didn't mean this! I didn't want this at all –

He turns way, and with a cry of fear and horror, runs out of the room.

No – no!

*The **Monster** stumbles forward and falls over the body of **Clerval** lying in his way. He recovers and kneels up, and runs his hands wonderingly over **Clerval**'s face – and then, as wonderingly, over his own. He looks up and around, seeing everything for the first time. Then, with heavy grace, he gets to his feet and moves towards the open door. He stops there – looks back once at **Clerval** – then goes out as **Clerval** stirs and groans.*

Clerval   Frankenstein – where are you …

Clerval pushes himself up and looks around. Seeing the empty bench, he staggers up, finds the trailing wire, and looks at the open door.

It's gone! – it's gone! Frankenstein … in God's name, what have you done?

He runs out. A final flash of lightning fills the window. The thunder crashes out and dies away as darkness falls.

Act 2

Inside a simple cottage in the forest. A rough table, a couple of rough chairs, a simple fireplace, a window overlooking some trees. It is neat and clean, but very simply furnished. On the table, the remains of a meal – some bread, an apple, a piece of cheese. Sunlight is streaming in through the window, and through the door upstage, through which we also see more trees. To one side, there is another door. Birds can be heard singing.

In the distance, there is the furious barking of dogs – like hounds in a hunt. It lasts for a short while and then dies away.

*Suddenly the light is blocked in the doorway. The **Monster** is standing there, panting. It is hard to tell what his expression is, though anger and fear seem to mingle in it. He is wearing a torn white shirt which is too small for him, and his hands and arms are torn and bloody.*

He stands there nervously for a moment, then makes up his mind and steps in, looking around as if for any threat.

Then he sees the food on the table and seizes it, devouring it ravenously, cramming the bread and cheese into his mouth and sniffing at the apple. His feet are clearly badly torn.

*Hearing something, the **Monster** freezes. It is a young man's voice, and a young girl's. During their exchange the **Monster** looks around desperately, sees the other door, makes for it, and gets through, shutting it behind him just before **Felix** and **Agathe** enter.*

Felix	*[Off]* Not far now. Mind that stone.
Agathe	*[Off]* Heavens above, Felix, I know there's a stone there. I know every inch of this path …
Felix	*[Off]* You ought to carry a stick. I don't know why you don't.
Agathe	*[Off]* What, and go tap-tapping everywhere? I need my hands to carry things in. I'm more agile than you are. And I bet I

could find my way back to the cottage from anywhere in these woods, I know them so well …

*They appear in the doorway, just as the **Monster** closes the other door.*

*They are young and simply dressed. **Felix** is carrying a musket and a dead rabbit. **Agathe** a basket of mushrooms. Although blind, she knows her surroundings so well that she moves around with great freedom.*

***Felix** stands the musket in the corner.*

Felix	There. I'll clean that this evening. Time I made some more bullets.

*He puts the rabbit on the table, but carelessly: he does not notice that the food has been eaten. **Agathe** puts her basket there too, and then sits down.*

Agathe	And I'll skin the rabbit in a minute. Shall I make a pie? Or would you like stew?
Felix	He's an old one – he'll be a bit tough. We'll have a stew, and put some of that wild garlic in.
Agathe	And the mushrooms and a carrot or two … we're living quite well. Who'd have thought we could?
Felix	Not the judges who sent us here, that's for sure. They thought exile would kill us, as it killed father.
Agathe	We'll survive. We'll do more than survive – we'll prosper.
Felix	We haven't faced winter yet. That won't be so easy … look, I think I'll load the gun before I go. Just in case.
Agathe	If you must. But don't expect me to shoot anyone.

*During the discussion, **Felix** loads his musket with powder and shot, while **Agathe** fetches and tunes a guitar from the corner of the room.*

Felix	I don't like leaving you alone without any protection. Just point it roughly in the right direction and pull the trigger – that's all you have to do.

29

Agathe	I don't like the noise.
Felix	All right, swing it round and hit 'em with it, I don't care. But I'll feel better if you have something to protect you, even if you're so brave and independent that you don't want it.

Felix uses the musket's ramrod to check that the bullet is firmly in place.

Agathe	Who's going to attack me, Felix?
Felix	That's a silly question. This is a wild part of the country, Agathe – there are wolves and bears in the forest, even if the bandits are having a day off. And there's been some kind of trouble down in the town. Didn't you hear the dogs earlier on?
Agathe	I thought the men were hunting …
Felix	The town dogs were barking too. You must have heard them.
Agathe	Well, if it's down in the town, you'll need the musket more than I will. Oh, I'm not arguing – I know you're right. But I feel safe here.
Felix	No harm in being prepared. If we didn't need more powder and lead I'd leave the rest of the stuff for a day or so, but I might as well get it all … what else was it? Flour?
Agathe	And soap, and salt. And if you can find some honey …
Felix	We could set up a hive or two ourselves next year. I wonder if I can find anyone who could let me have a queen bee?
Agathe	We'll be living like kings!
Felix	I suppose we could settle here … the people in the town are friendly enough, and I could get some kind of work on a farm, perhaps. But it's very lonely for you.
Agathe	Better than prison. Have you loaded that thing yet?
Felix	Just about. It's here in the corner. Remember, you pull back the hammer two clicks. And hold it tight, or you'll hurt yourself.

He stands the gun in the corner and shoulders a canvas bag.

Felix	I'll be back before sundown. D'you want some wood for the fire before I go?
Agathe	No, I'll do that. You go.

He kisses her.

Felix	I should get that rabbit cooking soon, or it'll be like eating a boot.
Agathe	Oh, stop fussing!

Laughing, he goes out.

She puts the guitar down and reaches on to the table for the apple. Feeling that it is not there, she frowns.

Oh, you might have left me the apple ... that's a mean trick.

Her hand finds the loaf, torn and half-eaten. She picks it up to feel it properly.

That's odd ... it was a fresh loaf.

She feels around for the cheese.

And where's the cheese? He hasn't taken that too? Felix, you greedy pig.

She gets up and goes to the door as if to call him back, but changes her mind.

Well, he's got a long way to go, and a lot to carry. But it's not like him to take it without saying anything ...

She comes back and sits down, picking up the guitar.

Anyway, I'm not hungry.

She plucks a chord – then stops abruptly.

Supposing it wasn't Felix, though?

Head alert, listening, she 'looks' around.

Hello? Is anyone there?

Silence.

The door was open … anyone could have come in … no, I'm being silly. This place is safe.

She begins to play a simple, folk tune.

*A few bars into it, the **Monster** silently appears. He merely stands and listens, as if he has never heard music before.*

She comes to the end of her short piece and puts the guitar down, sighing.

No … that's too sad. Oh, Papa …

*She gets up and wanders towards the **Monster**, who does not move, though he watches her carefully. Beside him on the wall is a picture: the portrait of an elderly man. She comes close and seems to be staring at it. The **Monster** is holding his breath, as if he is afraid of being discovered – and then he seems to realize that the girl cannot see him, and moves his hand slowly in front of her face, getting no reaction. A light dawns on his expression, but he does not move.*

Then she reaches up, takes the picture from the wall, and goes back to sit down. He stays where he is and listens.

Father, I expect it's silly talking to a picture I can't see – it's silly talking to a picture anyway. But I can't worry Felix, and I can't write a diary, and … I'm just worried, Papa. Will we survive here? Will we manage to find enough food? Will Felix find work somewhere? You're silent. You don't know any more than I do. Are you watching over us, Papa? I'm sure you would if you could. But we haven't done badly, have we? We never had to lift a finger before. The servants did it all for us. But we've lived here for six months now, and every so often Felix shoots a rabbit or a couple of pigeons, and there's the apple tree, and I know where the wild strawberries grow … I think you *are* looking after us, Papa. You wouldn't leave us on our own …

*During this speech, the **Monster** silently moves towards the door and goes out.*

She presses the picture to her heart, bowing her head over it.

But it's very hard ... I wish we'd said goodbye before they took you away. Though I don't know how I could have let you go ...

*The **Monster** returns. His arms are full of logs. As she sits still with her head bowed, he puts them down very carefully, so as not to make a noise, in the hearth.*

Then he takes an apple from his pocket and puts it on the table – only to freeze and draw his hand back as she looks up at where he is standing. He stands still as she gets up slowly and goes to put the picture back on the wall. Then she picks up a little mirror from the shelf.

Thank Heaven, I remember what you looked like, Papa ... I can judge a real face with my hands now, but I can't judge the expression of a picture. And I can't see my own face any more ... I used to be pretty. I *think* I was pretty. What I am now, only Felix knows ...

*She looks in the mirror. The **Monster**, who has come up silently beside her, watches curiously, comparing her face with the image.*

Then she puts the mirror back.

It's no good. Everything's changed; there's no point in looking back.

She goes to the fireplace and tries to pick up the basket of logs – but finds it full and feels them, surprised.

Oh! Felix, you've done it after all! But it's not like you to play tricks on me. Or – I wonder – the bread, the apple – *was* it Felix?

She gets up swiftly and goes to stand in the doorway, as if she is nervous about remaining inside. She looks out, biting a nail.

*Meanwhile the **Monster**, unable to resist it, picks up the mirror, feeling his own face, and slowly brings the glass up and looks in it.*

| Monster | Uggghhhh! |

He drops the mirror, which shatters. **Agathe** *hears, and turns at once in fear.*

Agathe	Who's that? Who's there?

He leaps to her and seizes her hand before she can run away.

Agathe *screams.*

He puts his hand over her mouth. She struggles, but he is too strong.

Monster	No! No! Friend!

With one hand he holds her, and with the other he reaches to the table and picks up the apple, which he puts into her hands. As she feels it he says again.

Monster	Friend! Friend!
Agathe	You're giving me an apple ... who are you? What do you want?

Seeing her relax a little, he releases her. She steps away at once, still fearful.

Monster	I have come ... a long way ... help. Help me.
Agathe	It was you that ate the bread – and brought the logs in?
Monster	I will not hurt anyone. I am their friend. Friend of everyone. I give you ...

He reaches for her hands and folds them around the apple again.

Not hurt anyone. Not kill, not hurt. Friend.

She releases her hands gently and puts the apple on the table.

Agathe	Let me ... please, I'm blind, you see ... may I feel your face? So I can tell what you look like?
Monster	You see with hands?
Agathe	It's the only way I can.
Monster	No. Not touch me. No.

He backs away as she reaches for him.

Agathe	But you can see what I look like.
	He shakes his head, turning away, as her hands reach up to his face.
Monster	No – not good, not good …
	Her hands are on his cheeks, his eyes, his mouth. Suddenly she pulls them away and steps back.
Agathe	I'm sorry …
Monster	I said *not good.*
Agathe	You poor man!
	He is puzzled.
Monster	Man?
Agathe	You must have suffered … What's your name?
Monster	No name. Please – you listen. I come a long way. I look for friends. I have no home. Men see me, they hurt me – dogs – they shout, they throw stones. But I am *good.* I want to love them, not hurt, not kill. I come here – I see house – I was hungry, I take food. Pardon. Forgive me. Everywhere I go, they hate me. Am I not good? I look bad. But I am good, I want to help and love – I help you? Bring you food, bring you wood? Please! My heart is unhappy – I stay here? You tell the man?
Felix	*[Calling, off]* Agathe – are you there?
Agathe	*[Calling]* Felix! Oh, Felix, listen to me –
	Felix runs in, sees the Monster apparently attacking her and Agathe apparently struggling to be free, and without hesitation seizes the musket.
Felix	Dear God! He's here –
Agathe	No, Felix! Don't! Don't shoot –
Monster	Tell him!
Agathe	Don't Felix!
Felix	Out of the way – Agathe, get *down* –

*But she turns to the **Monster** and clings to him, trying to shield him.*

Agathe	Felix, listen –

*The **Monster**, far stronger than she is, pushes her aside, and as she falls **Felix** shoots.*

*The roar of the musket fills the stage. The **Monster** staggers and cries out.*

Monster	AAAGGGGHHHHHHH!

Clutching his breast, he staggers to the door, where he clings to the frame.

Agathe	Felix! What have you done?
Felix	Are you hurt? What's he done to you?

*He runs to **Agathe** and helps her to sit up, but she pushes him away and feels for the **Monster**.*

Agathe	Oh, where are you? Where have you gone?
Felix	Agathe! What are you doing? For God's sake, keep away from him –

*She reaches the **Monster** and seizes his hand, but he thrusts her away.*

Monster	You *want* me bad! All of you – everyone – you all *want* me bad!
Agathe	No – no –

***Felix** runs to hold her and keeps her back from the **Monster**, who pulls himself up and looks at them both with a face twisted with hatred.*

Monster	Evil? Evil – you *want* evil? – then I shall be evil! I shall be terror and hatred and revenge – *revenge*!

With a mighty howl of anger, he runs off.

Agathe	Oh, Felix! What have you done?

Felix	You didn't see him, Agathe – and you don't know what he's done already! The villagers have been hunting him for days …
Agathe	*We* should have understood him, Felix. He was an outcast just like us. We could have helped him – he begged for it! What have you done to him now? Have you made him evil forever?

She pulls herself away from him and runs out. **Felix** *makes as if to follow, but stops and sits down in baffled defeat. A long way off we hear the* **Monster**.

Monster	*[Howling faintly, off]* Revenge! Revenge!

Act 3

Frankenstein's study in Geneva. The shape is the same as that of the room in Act One. There is no bench nor shelves of medical specimens; otherwise it is much the same. Frankenstein is sitting at his desk, his head resting on his arms.

The shutters are closed, and the room is lit by a lamp and by the flickering firelight.

After a moment or two, the door opens and Elizabeth comes in. Frankenstein looks up.

Frankenstein	Any news of William?
Elizabeth	No. One of the village girls saw him playing by the lake at four o'clock – she heard the clock chime, so she knew what time it was. He was on his own, under the trees. But, Victor, he's played there dozens of times! It's perfectly safe!
Frankenstein	I know, I know … he can't have gone far. I expect he'll turn up soon – he's bound to.

He gets up and opens the shutter to look out. It is dark outside.

Elizabeth sinks anxiously into a chair.

Elizabeth	Oh, what can have happened? Something's wrong, I know it, Victor! Did I tell you about my dreams?
Frankenstein	*[Still at the window]* Those dreams again?
Elizabeth	I can't get them out of my head. There's a monstrous figure – I can't see him clearly, but when he appears, there's such a sense of doom and horror that I wake up crying with fear – what can it mean, Victor?
Frankenstein	It means you need some laudanum to help you sleep. I'll give you some later.

Elizabeth	You don't think I'm going to sleep till they find William, do you?
Frankenstein	No. No, of course not … wait. There's someone down there. There's a group of them …

Elizabeth jumps up and runs to the window.

Elizabeth	It's the priest … What's he carrying? Oh, no – it can't be –

She clings to Frankenstein.

It's William – he's *dead* –

With a desperate cry, she runs from the room. Frankenstein sinks to his knees in despair.

Frankenstein	[Groans] Oh, dear God, this is my doing! I know who did this – why did I ever start this cursed thing?

Suddenly the window is flung open. Crouched on the sill, wearing a long, black cloak, his eyes blazing, is the Monster.

Monster	Frankenstein!
Frankenstein	Demon –

He springs at the Monster as if to kill him, but the Monster leaps lightly into the room and easily brushes him aside. Frankenstein falls, but jumps up again and grapples with him.

Frankenstein	Murderer! You did this, didn't you? You killed my brother! Monster! Vile thing!
Monster	I am exactly what you made me, Frankenstein.

They struggle together. There is a cry outside and the door handle turns.

The Monster lets Frankenstein go, sweeps the hood of the cloak up to cover his face, and sits down with his back to the door. Frankenstein staggers away and opens the door. Elizabeth is there. She clings to Frankenstein, weeping. He has to let her come in. She does not see the Monster.

Elizabeth	Strangled! He was killed, Victor … strangled … they found his little body down by the shore –

Frankenstein	Oh, no – no –
Elizabeth	What did he ever do to deserve that? He was the kindest little child – the sweetest little boy – he never hurt a … oh, Victor, it's too cruel! I can't bear it …

She sobs in his arms. He stands stiffly, conscious all the time of the **Monster***.*

Oh, Victor, come down – you must come and help me – I can't manage on my own – please Victor, I need you –

She stops suddenly. She has seen the **Monster***. A moment's petrified silence.*

Elizabeth	*[Screams]* Oh, Victor – what – who –
Frankenstein	Leave us, Elizabeth. I must talk to – my visitor. I'll come down in –
Elizabeth	But who is it? Oh, dear God, Victor, what are you doing? What have you done? Oh, am I going mad? I can't bear it –
Frankenstein	I'll explain everything, Elizabeth. But not now. I must talk to this gentleman. Believe me, it's desperately important.
Elizabeth	Victor, your little brother has been murdered! He's lying downstairs! Oh, can't I make you understand?

She runs to the **Monster** *and places a hand on his shoulder.*

Please, sir – you must make my cousin help me – tell him to come down with me and –

The **Monster** *turns to look at her. His hood falls back: she sees his face.*

Frankenstein	No!
Elizabeth	*[Screams]* The dream! The figure in the dream – Oh, God, help me –

She runs out. **Frankenstein** *moves helplessly as if to follow, but the* **Monster** *is on his feet, holding him back.*

Monster	Let her go. You must listen to me now and do as I say. The time for regrets is past.
Frankenstein	Monster! I didn't create you to do evil – why have you betrayed me?
Monster	I – betray *you*? If I knew how to laugh, Frankenstein, I'd shake the house with scorn. *You* are the betrayer – you created me, and you made sure I could never be happy. Isn't that betrayal?
Frankenstein	No! I swear it wasn't like that. I made you, yes –
Monster	And as soon as you saw what you'd done, you turned away in horror and left me to find my own way through the world – a creature everyone turned from with disgust and loathing – a vision from a nightmare! But do you know the cruellest thing of all? It was that I wanted to love. I came to life full of goodwill and friendship for every living creature – I wanted to help them and protect them and give them all the love I felt for them – and when I tried, they stoned me and shot at me and set their dogs on me – and even the dogs turned away in disgust … Frankenstein, has any man in history ever been more cruel than you have been to me?
Frankenstein	You killed my little brother! Is that love? Is that goodwill?
Monster	Listen! And I'll tell you everything.
	*He releases **Frankenstein**, who falls into the chair. The **Monster** walks up and down as he speaks; **Frankenstein** hides his head in his hands, occasionally looking up to reply – the very picture of despair.*
Monster	When I came to life I knew nothing. I didn't know who I was, I didn't know what the world was – things had no names. The only thing I knew was pain, but I didn't know that that was till much later, when I found out what it was called. Everything was new, Frankenstein. Do you know how beautiful things are when they're new? Or have you forgotten?
Frankenstein	Get on …

Monster	Ah, yes. I went down into the town, and they called out their dogs. Creatures full of beauty, with soft fur and bright eyes. I wanted to kneel down and pet them and play with them, but they tore at me with their teeth, and then I knew fear for the first time. I ran to the forest, where it was quiet, where there was cool water to bathe my flesh. The moon came up – oh, Frankenstein, to see the moon for the first time! And I found out what sadness was, and loneliness. Those other beings like myself – they stood upright, like me – they'd thrown stones and shouted harsh words at me, but they had companions, fellows, friends. Couldn't I find a friend? So I began to look …
Frankenstein	Where? Where did you look? And how did you learn to speak?
Monster	By listening. By hiding, and listening, and practising by myself. I found a cottage in the forest where a girl and her brother were living – a blind girl, the only piece of luck I ever had. She couldn't see me. We spoke together; oh, I would have been her slave, I would have helped them and worked for them, I would have done anything if they'd only accepted me – but her brother shot me with his musket as if I were a wild beast. It broke my arm. The bullet's still in my shoulder. That was when I found out what pain was really like. All alone in the icy mountains, weeping, crying with rage and loneliness – Frankenstein, you can't imagine how I suffered. If you could imagine it, you'd be on your knees praying to your God for forgiveness.
Frankenstein	My God?
Monster	Your God has nothing to do with me. You are my God. You made me, and you owe me happiness. Listen, and I'll tell you the last part of my story. When my wound healed, the bitterness and hatred ebbed away a little; I was still ready to love, still ready to trust … you see what you'd made, Frankenstein? A creature better than yourself, perhaps? A nature more noble? Who knows what might have happened if … well, I was more cunning by then. More cautious. I thought – it's only grown men and women who hate me; they've learned to be suspicious and to think the worst of people.

But if I could find a child, a little innocent creature with no hatred in its heart, then I could take it with me to the wilderness and bring it up as my companion – and we should love each other and live in peace and goodwill with all living creatures –

Frankenstein   No! No – not my brother –

Monster   Be silent.

At this point either in the darkness at the back of the stage, or from a trapdoor in the centre of it, a child silently appears. He is dressed in white, with a white expressionless mask, playing silently: the Ghost of William. **Frankenstein** *sees, and starts up, but the* **Monster** *holds him back.* **Frankenstein** *watches in horror as the* **Monster** *acts out with the child what he is describing, the child also miming.*

I found such a child – a creature like an angel, playing on his own beside the lake. I took his arm – oh, gently, Frankenstein, I had no wish to hurt him. I said, 'Come with me, little one' – and he looked at me, and he screamed. I said, 'No, hush, I shan't hurt you, but you must come with me' – and he said, 'I shall tell my brother, Herr Frankenstein! He'll punish you, ugly monster!'

Frankenstein   Oh, no – no –

Monster   I put my hands to his mouth to silence him, because I was afraid. And your name resounded through my head. You, the creator of my misery. You, the source of all my unhappiness. Frankenstein, a name to curse forever! And in that moment I thought – Frankenstein is my enemy and I can hurt him. I can destroy what is his. I can make him unhappy as he made me – and I killed your brother, and I laughed! Yes! The one time I have ever laughed. And now you must do something for me.

Frankenstein   Never! I shall destroy you –

He leaps at the **Monster**, *who easily pushes him away.* **Frankenstein** *falls to the floor.*

Monster	Not yet. Did you create me to be evil?
Frankenstein	No!
Monster	Did you intend me to be cursed and hated by all mankind?
Frankenstein	No, never –
Monster	Did you create me to be good – to be like human beings but stronger, nobler, kinder – to be an image of what humanity might be?
Frankenstein	Yes, I did. I intended all that. But –
Monster	Then finish what you have started! How can I be good alone? How can I love, when I'm met with nothing but hatred and disgust? Give me a creature like myself, Frankenstein! Give me a mate – a wife – a friend, and we shall leave you alone forever. We'll go far away from this country, we'll leave Europe altogether, we'll live in the desert or in the cold wilderness of the north – we can survive there where humans can't. But I must have a companion! Foxes – bears – wolves have their mates; every bird has its partner; even rats and mice have their nests, their homes, their families ... am I to be the only creature in the universe doomed to live alone? Frankenstein, that would be too cruel. Let me be the kind of creature you want me to be – loving, peaceful, harmless, gentle. Let me have someone to love – someone like myself. Make me a companion – make me a wife!

*Pause. **Frankenstein** gets up, walks to the window, and leans his head on the wall, as if in anguished thought.*

Frankenstein	You swear you'll go then, and not come back?
Monster	I swear it!
Frankenstein	God forgive me ... I'll do it. It was wrong of me to start; but it would be worse not to finish ... You can argue well, Monster.
Monster	At last! At last I can hope for something ... how long?
Frankenstein	Two years.

Monster	Two years!
Frankenstein	I'll have to start from the beginning again, you realize. At least this time I won't have to rely on lightning... I've got an electrical machine that's much more powerful than the old one. But I can't hurry the task. Do you want it done properly?
Monster	Of course. Of course, yes, take your time. I can wait. But in two years' time, I shall return.
Frankenstein	In two years' time, it will be ready. But if I hear of you before then, I shall destroy it, and that will be the end.
Monster	You'll hear nothing. I'll be out of sight, but I'll be watching.

He opens the window and springs on to the sill.

Two years, Frankenstein!

He leaps away.

Frankenstein sinks to the chair.

Frankenstein	What have I done? – And yet he was right, I must do it ...

A knock at the door, and Clerval enters, wearing a heavy overcoat.

Clerval	Frankenstein – I've just heard the news about your brother – my poor fellow! They're hunting the murderer with dogs. They'll find him, never fear.
Frankenstein	It's too late, Clerval. They won't find him ... out there.
Clerval	You think not? – But listen my friend, you must come down. Elizabeth needs you. There are things to be done ...

Frankenstein gets up wearily.

Frankenstein	Yes. You're right. Oh, Clerval, is there a curse on my family?
Clerval	A curse? No, no. Only bitter misfortune.

Frankenstein leaves. Clerval goes to follow him – sees the open window – goes to close it – looks out. He seems to be seeing the Monster disappearing in the distance, because he starts with surprise, looks at the door, makes as if to call after Frankenstein, then changes his mind and shakes his head.

No – it's a trick of the light. It's not possible. But I could have sworn – [*Calling*] Frankenstein! I'll come with you!

With a last worried look around, he goes out. Darkness falls.

Act 4

The same room, two years later. The main difference lies in the fact that there is a bench with a form on it covered by a sheet – the **Monster's Bride** – and, connected to it by all manner of complex wires and clips, a large electrical machine – similar to the small one we saw in Act One, but as tall as a man, and equipped with brass terminals.

The shutters are closed; the light is dim. After a moment, we hear a key turning in the lock, and then the door opens, and in come **Elizabeth** and **Clerval**. She is carrying a lamp.

He shuts the door carefully, after listening to make sure that no one is coming. She puts the lamp down on the table.

Elizabeth	We haven't got long – he'll be back in an hour or so. I feel like a traitor, like a spy …
Clerval	Don't. I'm as suspicious as you are, and I think I know …

He sees the sheeted form on the bench, which she still has not noticed. He helps her to sit down with her back to it.

I'm pretty sure I know what he's doing.

Elizabeth	But to keep the room locked for two years! And forbid anyone to come in! It's like Bluebeard's castle … Is he mad, Henri? He hasn't been the same since before William was killed. Since he went away to University, in fact.
Clerval	No, I don't think he's mad, Elizabeth. Not mad in the sense of incapable, anyway. He's a genius. He's the greatest man of science the world has ever seen …
Elizabeth	If you tell me that, then I believe you. But why is he so unhappy? He's like someone haunted by a demon. Surely a great genius should be happy with the work he's doing?

47

Clerval	Not if that work is like his.
Elizabeth	But what's he doing? What's he got in here? Why won't he let anyone in? I've thought of stealing his key and letting myself in dozens of times, but I was too afraid of what I'd find – and yet I couldn't imagine what it could be … Thank Heaven you came back from Ingolstadt, Henri.
Clerval	I think I know what he's doing. I only hope I can prevent him from doing it again. And I think I know who killed little William. Elizabeth, you must be brave.
Elizabeth	What do you mean? Surely not that Victor himself – but that's not possible! What is he doing?

She looks around wildly and sees the bench. She stands up suddenly.

What's that?

| Clerval | Don't look! I suspected this. Elizabeth, you mustn't touch it – |

He holds her back from going to look at it.

Elizabeth	Then tell me! Tell me what's going on, I beg you!
Clerval	Victor is creating life.
Elizabeth	Creating … I don't understand. Creating life? Now I think I'm going mad – what is that under there?
Clerval	Listen. When you came to his rooms in Ingolstadt, he'd just finished showing me an experiment – a horrible thing – with a hand – a human hand, taken from a dead body. He could animate it by passing electricity along the nerves. And more than that – he'd put together a complete creature – an artificial man. Do you remember the storm that night?
Elizabeth	I've never heard such thunder – oh, Henri, this is appalling – he's made a – a –
Clerval	A man, a being, and by attaching a wire to the roof he conducted electricity down from the lightning and … brought it to life. He didn't want me to see – at least, he was proud of

what he'd done, and wanted to show someone; but when it came to life I think he was as shocked as I was.

Elizabeth	And it did come to life?
Clerval	Oh, yes. And this is something I've never told anyone: I saw it on the afternoon William was killed. From this window – down by the lake, among the trees, just as night was falling – a monstrous figure leaping away into the darkness.

Elizabeth looks at the bench.

Elizabeth	His visitor ... The man I saw in his room!
Clerval	And that looks like another one.
Elizabeth	Oh, this is horrible!

She clings to him.

Clerval	Elizabeth, you must go downstairs. I'm going to destroy this thing. If he comes back while I'm here, you must keep him away.
Elizabeth	Yes – yes. He mustn't finish it. Oh, this is a nightmare ...

He opens the door for her.

Clerval	Remember – do all you can to keep him downstairs while I ... finish this.
Elizabeth	Yes. But what'll he do when he finds out?
Clerval	Then we'll have to talk to him. There must be some other way for him to use his gifts ...

*She goes out. He shuts the door and turns back to the bench, preparing himself for what lies under the sheet. He goes to the bench – takes the corner of the sheet as if to fling it aside – then hesitates, and looks around for something. Then he spots it: a large knife, like a cook's knife. He holds it up, testing the blade, and is about to pull the sheet aside when suddenly the shutters fly open with a crash. In the window, gigantic, enveloped in his cloak, is the figure of the **Monster**.*

Monster	Don't touch her!

*Clerval staggers back with a shock, and the **Monster** leaps down into the room.*

	He has sent you to do this?
Clerval	No! He doesn't know I'm here. It's my idea to destroy this thing, and I'll do it – and if I can, I'll destroy you too!
Monster	And that's humanity for you, in a nutshell. Stand away, man.

*Clerval makes as if to attack him, but the **Monster** easily brushes him aside.*

Monster	He made me too well. I'm disgusting to look at, I smell like the grave – but I'm too quick and too strong for you, Man, whoever you are. Where is Frankenstein now?
Clerval	On his way home.

*Another attack. This time **Clerval** falls, and the **Monster** bends down and snatches the knife from him.*

Monster	You'll never beat me like this. Why don't I kill you now? Why don't I snuff your life out like a candle? Shall I tell you? It's because he, cursed though he is, made me better than your God made you. It's because when I see a living thing I revere it – I want to cherish it and love it. When a human sees a living thing, his first impulse is to destroy it.
Clerval	That's not true!
Monster	Try living like me, and you'll soon find out how true it is.
Clerval	And the little boy?

*The **Monster** stands up and looks away.*

Monster	That's the one occasion when I behaved like a human being. As a result, it's the one thing I'm ashamed of.

*He goes back to the bench and pulls down the sheet to disclose the form of his **Bride**. She is chalk-white, with coarse black hair like his, dark lips, a red scar zigzagging down her face, as hideous as* *the **Monster**, in fact. She is dressed in a long white garment like a shroud. Her eyes are closed: she is not yet alive. As the **Monster** looks at her, he shudders and turns away for a moment; but then he makes himself look back.*

Monster	Beautiful … not like a human being. But we have our own beauty, she and I. Soon you'll wake up, my bride … soon we'll be together …
Clerval	A female –

Clerval comes to look, and recoils in horror.

Monster	A companion! Don't worry, *man*. We'll go off into the wilderness together, we'll live in peace and kindness –
Clerval	And what'll you do then? *Breed*?

*He springs to the electrical machine and tears out a handful of wires before the **Monster** can stop him.*

I'll never let it happen!

*The **Monster** roars with anger then leaps on **Clerval** and pulls him away from the machine, but **Clerval** pulls free and grabs another wire. He is about to tear it loose when the **Monster** strikes him down. He falls with a cry.*

Clerval	Aaaggghhhh!

*The loose end of the wire is still in his hand. The **Monster** strikes him again and again, until he is unconscious.*

Monster	Murderer! Destroyer! My bride – you've killed my bride –

*When **Clerval** is still, the **Monster** seizes the wire from his hand and stands in helpless agony, looking at the **Bride** and the loose wires that trail from the machine.*

Monster	You shall live! You *shall* live!

Feverishly he tries to connect the wires up again.

Where do they go? Where do they go? Frankenstein, Frankenstein!

*Suddenly the door bursts open. **Elizabeth** is standing there, together with a **Servant** holding two pistols.*

Elizabeth	There – *[gasping with shock as she sees the **Monster**]* ahhh!
Servant	In God's name, my lady – what is it?
Elizabeth	He's killed Monsieur de Clerval – shoot! Shoot!

*The **Servant** aims both pistols at the **Monster** and fires. The **Monster** staggers back with a cry.*

Monster	Aaaagggghhhh!

*Elizabeth runs to the body of **Clerval** and kneels beside him. The **Servant** tries hastily to reload – but the **Monster** recovers himself and leaps on him.*

Servant	No! No –
Monster	All killers – all destroyers – every one of you –

*He strikes the **Servant** down as he did **Clerval**. Pausing only to stare down at **Elizabeth** with feverish hatred, he springs back to the **Bride** and attaches the last wire to her head.*

Monster	My bride – awake! Awake!

*He starts to turn the handle of the great machine. **Elizabeth** watches in horror.*

Elizabeth	No! Don't do it.

*The terminals begin to spark and an electrical hum fills the air. Faster and faster, the **Monster** turns the wheel, groaning with effort. The electrical noise increases, sparks fly, but the **Bride** does not move.*

Monster	She's not moving – she's not coming alive – they've destroyed you! – No – wait – another wire –

Still turning the wheel with one hand, he reaches down and picks up the last loose wire. He looks with desperate urgency to see where it goes, then lets go of the wheel, which continues to turn of its own accord with the momentum, and bends down to slip his arm under her shoulders. He lifts her up, with the wire in his other hand -

brings the wire down to touch her heart – and suddenly she convulses into life with a terrifying scream.

Elizabeth
Oh no! No!

*She crouches in fear as the **Monster** and his **Bride** cling together in a desperate embrace, surrounded by sparks and a powerful humming and crackling.*

Monster
[Howling] Live! Live!

*The **Bride** cries out. Suddenly the door is flung open. **Frankenstein** stands there, looking around with horror.*

Frankenstein
Clerval! Oh no – Elizabeth!

Elizabeth
Victor – stop them! Stop them!

***Frankenstein** leaps to the machine. The **Monster**, still holding the **Bride**, cannot stop him as he pulls out handfuls of wires, scattering sparks everywhere and making the strange light from the machine surge, fade, and flicker.*

Monster
No! No – she's mine – she's alive –

*The **Bride** suddenly throws her arms up straight, her fingers clutching at the air, and then falls lifeless in his arms.*

Frankenstein
Never! She'll never live now! Monster, what have you done?

*The **Monster** looks down at her with horror and then lowers her gently on to the bench.*

Monster
What have I done, you say? Nothing – compared to what I'm going to do …

*Before **Frankenstein** can stop him, the **Monster** leaps towards **Elizabeth** and seizes her by the throat.*

Elizabeth
No! Help – Victor –

Frankenstein
Put her down! Don't do it –

*The **Monster**, with horrible snarls of rage, strangles her and drops her lifeless on the floor, then stands laughing as **Frankenstein** throws himself to his knees beside her.*

Frankenstein	Elizabeth – no – no …
Monster	Well, Frankenstein? Your sufferings have begun. How does it feel?
Frankenstein	Demon! Vile thing – destroyer!
Monster	Yes. Destroyer I shall be. I shall destroy *you*, my creator.

Frankenstein leaps at him – but he avoids him, and taunts Frankenstein from the window.

Monster	You'll follow me, Frankenstein. Wherever I go you'll come stumbling after me, intent on putting me to death – but you won't catch me!

Frankenstein runs at him again – and again fails to grasp the Monster.

Monster	I'll lead you to the ends of the earth – I'll make you follow me to the coldest, wildest, emptiest places in the world! I'll see you freeze and starve and suffer – and I'll laugh as you crawl through the barren mountains, the deserts, the ice-fields …
Frankenstein	I'll find you. However long it takes me, I'll follow you to the ends of the earth, and when I do, I'll tear you apart!
Monster	It'll take you as long as you live. Frankenstein, your sufferings are just beginning!

He leaps through the window and vanishes. **Frankenstein** *kneels again and takes up the body of* **Elizabeth** *in his arms.*

Frankenstein	What have I done? What have I done?

Bows over her, sobbing. The lights go down.

Epilogue

*Enter **Captain Walton** dressed as in the Prologue.*

*During **Walton's** speech, the lights slowly fade up to the same intense brightness as they reached during the Prologue.*

Captain Walton So that was the story Frankenstein told me. When he came to the end, he fell back exhausted, near to death. I left him in the care of one of my men, and went out on deck to breathe the cold air and think for a while about the incredible things I'd heard. But I hadn't been there for long when there was a cry from below. I ran down to the cabin – and saw the Monster crouching on the window-ledge. I shrank away in fear, but the Monster didn't move – for Frankenstein himself lay dead below him. The effort of telling his story had been too much. The creature looked at me and said 'It's ended, then. It's over.' I said 'And what will you do now?' He looked out at the waste of snow and ice, and said, 'I shall go north until I can go no further, and then I'll set fire to my sledge and lie down in the flames until my bones have turned to ash. They tell me that human beings have something called a soul that lives on after their bodies die. I hope I have no soul. All I want now is oblivion …' Then he turned and leapt down on to the ice, and drove his sledge away at a furious pace. A minute later he had vanished in the sunlight and the silence.

For a moment there is bright light – and then darkness falls at once.

Activities

ACTIVITIES

FRANKENSTEIN

KEY STAGE 3 FRAMEWORK OBJECTIVES	RELEVANT ACTIVITIES CHAPTER(S)
Sentence Level	
8 Starting paragraphs	Murder!
9 Main point of paragraphs	Murder!
11 Sentence variety	Murder!
12 Sequencing paragraphs	Murder!
Word level	
14 Word meaning in context	Planning a Horror Story
15 Dictionary and thesaurus	Planning a Horror Story
Reading	
1 Locate information	Frankenstein on Trial
4 Note-making	Frankenstein on Trial
Writing	
1 Drafting process	Planning a Horror Story; Murder!
5 Story structure	Planning a Horror Story
2 Planning formats	Characters in Freeze-frame
6 Characterisation	Characters in Freeze-frame; Planning a Horror Story; Murder!
7 Narrative devices	Planning a Horror Story
8 Link writing and reading	Planning a Horror Story
9 Link writing and reading	Characters in Freeze-frame; Murder!
Speaking and Listening	
1 Clarify through thought	Characters in Freeze-frame; Frankenstein on Trial
3 Shape a presentation	On the Stage
4 Answers, instructions, explanations	On the Stage
5 Put a point of view	Frankenstein on Trial
6 Recall main points	Frankenstein on Trial
7 Pertinent questions	Frankenstein on Trial
10 Report main points	Frankenstein on Trial
11 Range of roles	Frankenstein on Trial
12 Exploratory thought	Characters in Freeze-frame; Frankenstein on Trial
13 Collaboration	On the Stage
14 Modify views	Characters in Freeze-frame; Frankenstein on Trial; On the Stage
15 Explore in role	Improvise a New Scene; Frankenstein on Trial; Drama Techniques
16 Collaborate on scripts	Improvise a New Scene; Characters in Freeze-frame; Drama Techniques
17 Extend spoken repertoire	Improvise a New Scene; Frankenstein on Trial
18 Exploratory drama	Drama Techniques
19 Evaluate presentations	Improvise a New Scene; Characters in Freeze-frame; On the Stage

KEY STAGE 3 FRAMEWORK OBJECTIVES	RELEVANT ACTIVITIES CHAPTER(S)
Sentence level	
6 Grouping sentences	Murder!
7 Cohesion and coherence	Murder!
Word level	
7 c) Words in context	Planning a Horror Story
Reading	
3 Notemaking formats	Characters in Freeze-frame; Frankenstein on Trial
Writing	
1 Effective planning	Planning a Horror Story; Murder!
2 Anticipate reader reaction	Planning a Horror Story; Murder!
5 Narrative commentary	Planning a Horror Story
6 Figurative language	Planning a Horror Story
7 Establish the tone	Characters in Freeze-frame; Murder!
Speaking and Listening	
3 Formal presentation	Frankenstein on Trial; On the Stage
5 Questions to clarify or refine	Frankenstein on Trial; On the Stage
7 Listen for a specific purpose	Frankenstein on Trial; On the Stage
10 Hypothesis and speculation	Characters in Freeze-frame; Frankenstein on Trial; On the Stage
11 Building on others	Characters in Freeze-frame; Frankenstein on Trial
14 Dramatic techniques	Improvise a New Scene; Drama Techniques
15 Work in role	Improvise a New Scene; Characters in Freeze-frame; Frankenstein on Trial; ; Drama Techniques
16 Collaborative presentation	Improvise a New Scene; Characters in Freeze-frame; Drama Techniques

A Note to Teachers
If you choose to work through the Activities chapter 'On the Stage' with your class, remember to avoid 'A Note on Staging' (on pages 6 and 7) during preliminary work on the text.

ACTIVITIES   FRANKENSTEIN

Improvise a New Scene

In the playscript, the Monster describes himself as 'a creature everyone turned from with disgust and loathing – a vision from a nightmare!' He explains to Frankenstein how he tried to make friends, but how 'they stoned me and shot at me and set their dogs on me'.

In Mary Shelley's novel, the Monster describes how he rescued a girl from a fast-flowing river, but how he was repaid for his kindness with hostility and violence.

In groups, improvise a scene where the Monster tries to make friends by performing a kindness, but the people turn on him out of fear and ignorance. Remember:

● the Monster is lonely and wants friends
● he is strong and powerful, but he does not always use his full strength against people
● the people are scared of his strength, as well as his looks
● when people are scared, they often act like bullies
● not everyone always follows the crowd. The bravest people sometimes go against the majority, even if it makes them unpopular.

Ask for feedback from the class to help evaluate your presentation.

Characters in Freeze-frame

In Act 2, the Monster befriends Agathe, but they are interrupted by Felix, who believes the Monster is attacking his sister.

1   Imagine this scene (from page 34 onwards) is being filmed and choose a moment to 'freeze' a frame.

    1   Sketch the freeze-frame, showing the positions of the characters and the setting.

    2   Next to each character draw a large thought bubble. Think carefully about the emotions that each character might be feeling. Write their thoughts in the bubbles.

    3   Choose a character and think about how their thoughts might be shown through their body language and facial expression.

    4   Mime a couple of seconds in role as your chosen character. Ask a partner to guess who you are and what you are thinking.

2   If Felix had listened to Agathe, the scene might have ended very differently. In small groups, discuss:

- what Agathe could have said to make Felix listen
- how Felix might have reacted at first and how his reactions might have changed as Agathe and the Monster explained further
- what the Monster might have said to Felix
- what the outcome of the scene might be
- if Agathe and Felix were sympathetic to the Monster, how the story might end a) happily, and b) sadly.

3   When you and your partner (or group) have reached agreement, write out a script to end Act 2. Remember to:

- include a few brief stage directions
- focus on what the characters say to each other.

4   You may wish to act out your scene, to test how effective it is. Ask for comments from the rest of the class.

Planning a Horror Story

Frankenstein, the novel, was written by Mary Shelley when she was only 19. She was on holiday in Switzerland with her husband and some friends. The weather was so bad that they were forced to stay indoors, where they entertained each other by reading and making up horror stories.

For many days, Mary could not think of a story, but one night she had a nightmare – about a hideous creature brought to life by a scientist. The next day she got up and began writing her story: 'It was on a dreary night in November...'*

1 Plan a short horror story of your own, using the same opening words as Mary Shelley. Think about:

● **Setting**
   What are the classic horror settings? Somewhere remote, a hostile environment, savage weather, darkness, etc. Use metaphors and similes to enhance the descriptions.

● **Characters**
   Sometimes, evil characters are most interesting if they contain some good or appealing aspects. Think about how the good parts of your character can be overcome by the evil parts – perhaps by a single tragic event. The Monster in *Frankenstein* was 'born' good, but driven to evil because he was rejected and lonely.

● **Plot**
   Suspense is an important part of a horror story. It can be created by mystery, things unexplained, and a sense of danger that increases and follows a potential victim, relentlessly. Look up the word 'menace' in a dictionary and thesaurus. How can you convey this sense in your story?

* In her final version of the tale, Mary Shelley used these words at the beginning of the chapter in which the Monster finally comes to life.

Ensure that your story has a strong beginning, a complication leading to a crisis, and a resolution.

- **Themes**

  The most interesting stories have several themes or ideas running through them. Some of the main themes of *Frankenstein* are:

    - whether man-made objects can (or should) be brought to life
    - the struggle between good and evil
    - the need for friendship/partnership
    - life/death
    - visual appearance/blindness.

  Decide on themes that interest you and weave them into your story.

2   When you are satisfied with your plan, draft the story in full then give it to a partner to comment on. Revise the story in the light of their comments, then proofread your story and write out a final version.

Murder!

1   The following extract is from the novel. The narrator
    is the Monster, describing the death of William.
    However, the paragraphs are in the wrong order. Read
    them carefully, then put them in their proper sequence.
    Remember to look carefully at the opening of each
    paragraph and decide how it links with the previous
    paragraph.

1   It was evening when I arrived, and I retired to a hiding-place among the
    fields that surround it … I was oppressed by fatigue and hunger, and far
    too unhappy to enjoy the gentle breezes of evening, or the prospect of the
    sun setting behind the stupendous mountains for Jura.

2   He struggled violently. 'Let me go,' he cried; 'Monster! Ugly wretch! You
    wish to eat me, and tear me to pieces—You are an ogre. Let me go, or I
    will tell my papa.'

3   Urged by this impulse, I seized on the boy as he passed, and drew him
    towards me. As soon as he beheld my form, he placed his hands before
    his eyes, and uttered a shrill scream: I drew my hand forcibly from his
    face, and said, 'Child, what is the meaning of this? I do not intend to hurt
    you; listen to me.'

4   At this time a slight sleep relieved me from the pain of reflection, which
    was disturbed by the approach of a beautiful child, who came running
    into the recess I had chosen, with all the sportiveness of infancy.
    Suddenly, as I gazed on him, an idea seized me, that this little creature was
    unprejudiced, and had lived too short a time to have imbibed a horror of
    deformity. If, therefore, I could seize him, and educate him as my
    companion and friend, I should not be so desolate in this peopled earth.

5   'Boy, you will never see your father again; you must come with me.'

6   The child still struggled, and loaded me with epithets which carried
    despair to my heart. I grasped his throat to silence him, and in a moment
    he lay dead at my feet.

7   'Hideous monster! let me go. My papa is a Syndic—he is M. Frankenstein—he will punish you. You dare not keep me.'

8   'Frankenstein! you belong then to my enemy—to him towards whom I have sworn eternal revenge; you shall be my first victim.'

2   Re-read the second part of Act Four in the playscript (starting when Elizabeth and the servant burst through the door, page 52).

Re-write this section as a narrative, using the Monster as the narrator. Remember:
● to start a new paragraph when there is a shift of topic, viewpoint, time, or when there is a new speaker
● to use the first sentence to introduce the paragraph or move the action on
● to vary the structure of your sentences to give pace and variety
● that in a first-person narrative you may include the thoughts and feelings of the narrator, but not of the other characters
● you may wish to condense or cut out some of the speech in the playscript.

Swap your first draft with a partner and ask for comments. Is the text fluent? Does it make sense? Is it exciting? Redraft your narrative, in the light of his or her comments. Remember to check your spelling and punctuation, particularly the speech punctuation.

Frankenstein on Trial

1   What do you understand by the word 'tragic'? Note down your ideas, then look up the word in a dictionary and/or thesaurus. Is 'tragic' a good description of the story of *Frankenstein*?

2   There are three murders in the play (four, including the destruction of the Bride). Who is responsible for them? Although the Monster commits the murders, is it he or is it his creator, Frankenstein, who is truly guilty?

3   Put Frankenstein 'on trial' in the classroom.

Step 1

Divide into two groups: one group should be the prosecution (i.e. accuse Frankenstein of being guilty); the other group should be the defence (i.e. claim that Frankenstein is innocent).

Step 2

Each group should prepare their case. Consider the following:

- is it right that scientists should try to create life
- was it right for Frankenstein to create a companion for the Monster
- did Frankenstein have the right to destroy the Bride
- could Frankenstein have controlled his Monster, Could he have prevented the murders
- was Frankenstein right to use corpses in his work
- why did the university stop helping Frankenstein with his research?

Step 3

Skim the playscript for quotations that could be used at the trial. Make a note of them.

' you're not what I thought you'd be...
I thought I was making an angel!'

' It was wrong of me to start; but it would be worse not to finish...'

'Monster! I didn't create you to do evil – why have you betrayed me?'

Step 4

One member of the defence group should volunteer to be Frankenstein at the trial. He or she should stand at the front of the class and answer all questions in role.

Step 5
A spokesperson from the prosecution should put forward the group's views and questions.

Step 6
A spokesperson from the defence should put forward the group's views and questions.

Step 7
A judge (the teacher or a pupil) must sum up the arguments for and against Frankenstein.

Step 8
The whole class should now act as a jury and vote on whether Frankenstein is innocent or guilty.

Note: Alternatively, the Monster could be put on trial.

Drama Techniques

COMING TO LIFE

By the end of the play, the Monster is strong and agile. He feels great emotions and can describe his thoughts and feelings. But imagine what his 'awakening' felt like.

Work in pairs, with one person giving the instructions below and the other following them. Then swap roles.

1   Lie down, on your back, stretched out.
2   Lie completely still, close your eyes, and do not speak. Try to think of nothing but a black space.
3   Think about sound. What might you first hear as you wake up in Frankenstein's room?
4   Think about how your body might feel, lying on a wooden bench.
5   Think about what you might smell.
6   Think about what you might first see when you open your eyes.
7   Which part of your body might you move first?
8   What emotions might you feel? Fear? Curiosity? Happiness?

BEING BLIND

In the play, most people are revolted and frightened by the Monster's appearance (including his creator, Frankenstein), so they act with hostility and violence. Agathe is the only person who shows the Monster any sympathy and kindness. She is not horrified by the Monster's appearance because she cannot see him. Her blindness actually makes her more 'clear-sighted' in some ways.

1   Think about portraying Agathe onstage. Discuss:
   ● any senses that might be 'sharper' to compensate for her blindness
   ● how she can move about her home, despite being blind

- how her body language might be different from that of the other characters, e.g. how she might stand before the Monster; how she might incline her head to hear other characters speak.

2 Wear a blindfold and work through the following activities to help you understand how a blind person senses the world.

   1 Feel some objects as they are put into your hands and guess what they are.
   2 Try to walk across the room.
   3 Identify people by feeling their faces.
   4 Go on a walk with a sighted person. First, let them guide you by touch. Then, let them guide you just by speech.

3 Act out the early part of Act Two, paying particular attention to the portrayal of Agathe.

On the Stage

There are three settings in this play (apart from the Prologue and Epilogue, which could be staged with bright spotlighting on Captain Walton):

- Frankenstein's room in Ingolstadt
- the cottage belonging to Felix and Agathe
- Frankenstein's study in Geneva.

1   In groups of three, skim through the text, and make notes on the different settings and props you might need for each scene. Complete the grid below:

Room in Ingolstadt	Cottage	Study in Geneva
high arched windows	table	books
lamp	2 chairs	
	door	

2   When your table is complete, discuss your findings and decide what features of the set can be common to all three scenes.

3   Using this list, design a common set and decide how you could adapt it simply to show a change of scene, e.g. by lighting, by sound effects, by the addition of certain props, etc.

4   Working together, draw the basic set. Make three copies of it.

5   Divide the different settings between you, so that each member of your group has a different one. Working individually now, work up the basic set, showing how it

could be adapted to suit one particular setting and adding notes about lighting, sound effects, and props.

6   As a group again, present your three settings to the class, explaining how the stage could be adapted through the play.

Invite questions and comments from the class. You may wish to modify your sets in the light of this feedback.

7   Look carefully at the photographs below. They are scenes from performances of *Frankenstein*. Can you identify which scenes they are? Which lines do you think the actors might be saying?

Further Activities

1   Investigate other stories about people who have suffered because of disfigurement or deformity, e.g. *The Hunchback of Notre Dame*, *The Phantom of the Opera*, *The Elephant Man*. Find out whether they are based on the lives of real people.

2   *Frankenstein* has been a popular story ever since it was published. Many film versions have been made, e.g. *Frankenstein*, by Edison Films, 1910; *Frankenstein*, 1931, starring Boris Karloff. Try to find some film versions and compare how the Monster is portrayed in each film.

3   In both the playscript and the novel, the story is told 'inside another story'. Both begin and end with a narration by Captain Walton. What does this 'outside' narrative add to the play and novel? Find other stories that use a variety of narrators and compare their effects.

4   Find out what is meant by a 'gothic novel'. Mary Shelley wrote *Frankenstein* at a time when gothic novels were popular. How far do you think *Frankenstein* could be described as a gothic novel?

5   Scientific progress means that we can now help to create life, sustain life for longer, and even alter our appearance (through surgery). Some scientific progress causes great debate; for example, the development of cloning and the preservation of embryos. Find out more about one of these issues and write about the arguments for and against it.